# EXPLORATION OF NORTH AMERICA
## *Coloring Book*

Peter F. Copeland

DOVER PUBLICATIONS, INC., *New York*

# Introduction

European discovery of the New World and its Native American cultures may have come about accidentally even before the Vikings, but it is only with them, about 1000 A.D., that we have firm evidence. The Vinland adventure itself led nowhere, and it was only after Columbus' voyages that the Atlantic was constantly plowed by expeditions from numerous European nations, all laying claims to possession of territory.

European involvement in North America went through various illusionary phases before the land was recognized and exploited for what it was. Columbus and his immediate successors thought it was an outlying section of East Asia, the goal of their voyages. After this was disproved, the new continent was regarded mainly as an obstruction on the way to the rich markets of Asia, but not an unbroken one: for a long time explorers sought an easy sea passage through various parts of the north and the far west. Even Coronado and de Soto, the first Europeans to make deep inroads into the landmass and to recognize its extent, were blinded by hopes of finding once again the wealth of Mexico and Peru. Finally, the true riches of field, river, mountain and forest invited permanent settlement.

The present book includes the very first (or extremely early) European visits to the Caribbean (Columbus) and Mexico (Cortés), various parts of Canada (Vikings, Cabot, Cartier, Frobisher, Davis and others), the U.S. Southeast (Ponce de León, de Soto), the U.S. middle Atlantic coast (Verrazano, Ayllón), the U.S. Northeast (Verrazano, Gomes), Texas and the Southwest (Cabeza de Vaca, Coronado), California (Drake, Cabrillo), the Mississippi (de Soto, Marquette, La Salle) and Alaska (Bering).

It was not until after the American Revolution that the continent was completely traversed (Mackenzie, Lewis and Clark, Fraser) and that some of its remoter corners were investigated (Pike, Jedediah Smith). At this point (about 1830) our chronological survey ends.

Also included, alongside actual discoveries, are a number of important colonizations and settlements of already discovered areas: Roanoke, Jamestown, Quebec, Santa Fe, Plymouth, St. Mary's (Maryland) and Boonesborough (Kentucky).

---

Copyright © 1992 by Dover Publications, Inc.
All rights reserved under Pan American and International Copyright Conventions

Published in Canada by General Publishing Company, Ltd., 30 Lesmill Road, Don Mills, Toronto, Ontario.

Published in the United Kingdom by Constable and Company, Ltd., 3 The Lanchesters, 162–164 Fulham Palace Road, London W6 9ER.

*Exploration of North America Coloring Book* is a new work, first published by Dover Publications, Inc., in 1992.

DOVER *Pictorial Archive* SERIES

*International Standard Book Number: 0-486-27123-4*

Manufactured in the United States of America
Dover Publications, Inc., 31 East 2nd Street, Mineola, N.Y. 11501

**The Vikings in Vinland, ca. 1000 A.D.** The first European presence in North America for which there is reliable evidence occurred in 986, when a Viking ship from Greenland (discovered and colonized only a few years earlier) was blown off course and accidentally discovered the new land. Around the year 1000, another Greenland Viking, Leif Eiriksson, landing perhaps on Labrador or Newfoundland, called the place Vinland from the profusion of wild grapes growing there. Later Leif's brother Thorvald established a colony there. He and his crew spent two years exploring the coast and fighting the natives (either Indians or Eskimos), who eventually forced the Vikings to abandon the Vinland settlement and return to Greenland. Further attempts at settlement, all unsuccessful, extended perhaps as late as 1020.

**Columbus' *Niña* in the Bahamas, 1492.** On October 12, 1492, after a 70-day voyage from Spain, Christopher Columbus, bearing a commission from the Spanish crown to reach Asia by sailing west, arrived with his three ships *Niña*, *Pinta* and *Santa María* in the Bahama Islands. Claiming the islands for Spain, he then discovered Cuba and Hispaniola (now Haiti and the Dominican Republic). This was the crucial voyage that opened the New World to European exploration and settlement. Columbus made three more voyages to the Caribbean, in 1493, 1498 and 1502, landing in the Virgin Islands, Puerto Rico, Guadeloupe, Antigua, Jamaica and Trinidad; touching on the mainland of Central America, at Panama and Honduras; and exploring the mouth of the Orinoco River in Venezuela.

**John Cabot explores Canada's east coast, 1497.** The Italian-born John Cabot (Giovanni Caboto) made voyages to North America in the service of England in 1497 and 1498, during which he explored the coasts of Newfoundland, Labrador and probably Maine; he was lost on the 1498 voyage. His son Sebastian was involved in further English ventures and claimed to have made a voyage to America about 1509, searching for a northwest passage to Asia; some believe he may have reached Hudson Bay. These voyages opened to European fishing fleets the cod fisheries on the Grand Banks of Newfoundland. (In the illustration, the little *Matthew*, John Cabot's 1497 vessel, is dwarfed by the cliffs and crags of the Newfoundland coast.)

**João Fernandes explores the coast of Greenland, 1499.** The King of Portugal, learning of John Cabot's voyages, sponsored several expeditions into northern waters. On one of these, João Fernandes explored the coast of Greenland, which had long been abandoned by the original Viking colonists. Perhaps chagrined by the king's sponsorship of Corte-Real, Fernandes entered the service of England and was probably lost on an English expedition in 1502.

**Corte-Real explores Newfoundland, 1500.** In 1500 the Portuguese explorer Gaspar Corte-Real explored the shores of Newfoundland and Labrador, possibly discovering the Gulf of St. Lawrence. He was lost at sea in a second voyage in 1501. The survivors returned to Portugal with 57 native inhabitants of these regions. (Here we see Corte-Real's flagship preparing to launch a boat along a fog-shrouded northern shore littered with the debris of a melting iceberg.)

**Ponce de León explores Florida, 1513.** In the spring of 1513, Juan Ponce de León, the Spanish conqueror of Puerto Rico, set sail from that island with three ships in search of the fabulous island of Bimini, where, according to legend, a magic fountain promised perpetual youth to those who partook of it. During Easter week he got his first look at the mainland of what is now the United States. He called the new land Florida after the Spanish name for Easter, and claimed it for the Spanish crown. Hostile natives confined the Spanish to only a few landings along the coast, as they sailed south to Cape Canaveral. Struggling against the powerful Gulf Stream (hitherto unknown), the Spanish ships made their way along the Florida Keys and went up the west coast into the Gulf of Mexico, then turned back for home. In 1521, Ponce de León returned, hoping to conquer Florida for the King of Spain. Though he commanded two well-armed ships, carrying 250 soldiers and 50 horses, upon landing in Florida he was driven off by the natives and so seriously wounded that he died in Havana a few days later.

6

**A Basque whaler off the Grand Banks of Newfoundland, 1520s.** Basque whalers from the old kingdom of Navarre in Spain were fishing off Newfoundland by the 1520s, and in increasing numbers thereafter. Once killed, the whales were towed ashore, where their oil was boiled out in big iron cauldrons. It has been claimed that the Basques had been fishing the Newfoundland waters for cod before John Cabot's voyage of 1497, and there are legends that they were on the Grand Banks even before 1492. In 1578 an English observer stated that he saw 100 Basque vessels there fishing for cod and 30 to 40 more killing whales. Basque whalers in the waters off Newfoundland undertook the first long-distance whaling voyages by European seamen.

**Cortés and Montezuma, 1519.** The conquest of Mexico and the overthrow of the great Aztec empire of Montezuma (Motecuhzoma II) was accomplished by Hernán Cortés, coming from Cuba with an army of a few hundred men and 16 horses. Aided psychologically by an Indian legend that suggested Cortés was an ancient Mexican god returned to earth, and physically by their steel weapons, armor and war-horses, the Spanish won many of the Aztecs' native subjects as allies. The Aztec emperor was taken prisoner by Cortés and stoned to death by his own people while the Spanish fought desperate battles with the Aztecs in and around the capital. In 1521 the city fell to Cortés, and the Spanish were in control of Mexico, which they renamed New Spain.

**Verrazano explores the middle Atlantic coast, 1524.**
King Francis I of France now entered the competition to discover a short route to the East Indies. He commissioned Giovanni Verrazano of Florence to undertake a voyage of exploration to the New World. Verrazano arrived at the Carolina coast in 1524 with his ship the *Dauphine* and a crew of 50 men. First they sailed south searching for a passage or strait leading into the Pacific, then turned north up the Virginia and Maryland coasts to Delaware and on, exploring what would one day become New York harbor. From there Verrazano sailed north to Cape Cod and Maine, and finally to Newfoundland, from where he returned home.

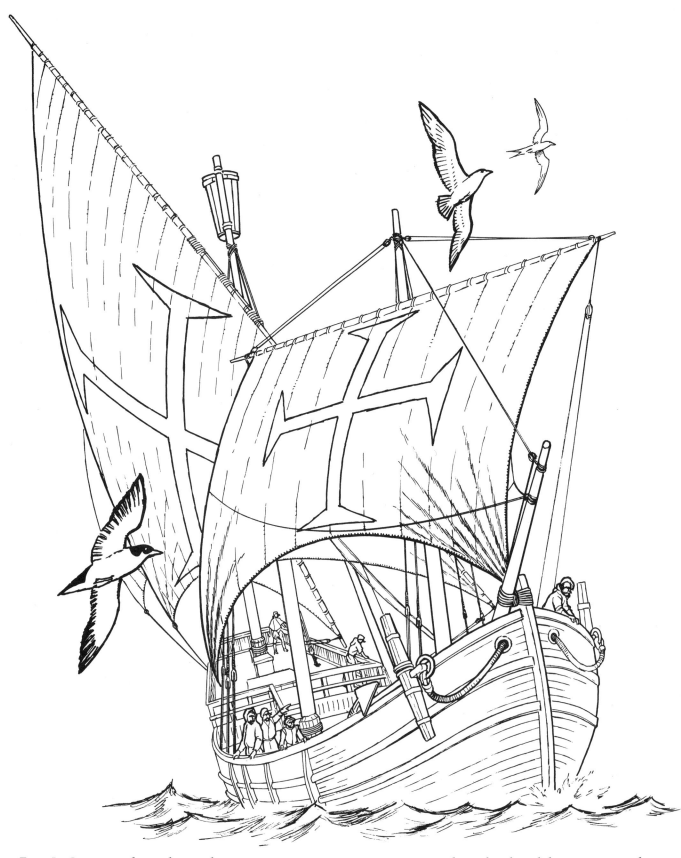

**Estevão Gomes explores the northeast coast, 1525.** In 1524 King Charles I of Spain commissioned the Portuguese-born Estevão Gomes to scout the entire northeast coast of the continent to discover a short sailing route through North America to the Spice Islands of the East Indies. Gomes sailed a 75-ton ship from Spain to Cuba, and then along the coast from New England to Nova Scotia for seven months. He failed to find a western passage to the Indies but did capture 58 Indians, taking them back to Spain with him in the hope of selling them as slaves. However, the King ordered their release. The information brought back by Gomes, and later by the associates of Ayllón, helped Spanish mapmakers draw charts of the east coast of North America from Florida to Newfoundland.

**Ayllón explores the Carolina coast, 1526.** In 1526 Lucas Vásquez de Ayllón brought a company of 600 people—European men and women and enslaved Africans—in two large vessels in order to establish a Spanish colony on the Carolina coast, probably near Cape Fear River. (He had commissioned two preliminary voyages of exploration, in 1521 and 1525.) This was the first introduction of African slavery into the territory of what was to become the United States. Ayllón died of a fever on the Carolina coast, the African slaves revolted and some of the settlers were killed fighting hostile Indians. In 1527 the colony was abandoned and the colonists returned to Hispaniola.

**Cabeza de Vaca travels through the southwest, 1528–36.** Álvar Núñez Cabeza de Vaca was a member of an expedition of 400 men from Cuba led by Pánfilo de Narváez which landed on Florida's west coast in 1528, searching for gold and conquest in the lands north of Mexico. On a long and terrible march into the interior, they suffered starvation and found themselves under constant Indian attack. Only Cabeza de Vaca and three other members of the expedition survived to reach an island near Galveston, Texas. They traveled across Texas, New Mexico and Arizona, finally reaching the Gulf of California after covering more than two-thirds of the distance across what was to become the United States of America. Cabeza de Vaca later served his country in South America and Africa.

**Cartier explores the Gulf of St. Lawrence, 1534.** King Francis I of France instructed Jacques Cartier to "discover certain islands and lands where it is said a great quantity of gold and other precious things are to be found." Cartier made three voyages to Canada between 1534 and 1542, during which he explored the Gulf of St. Lawrence and penetrated the St. Lawrence River beyond the present-day city of Quebec. (Here we see Cartier's flagship in heavy weather off the Canadian coast.)

**Coronado explores the Southwest, 1540–42.** In 1540 the legend of the Seven Cities of Gold caused the viceroy of Mexico to send out a substantial expedition headed by Francisco Vásquez de Coronado. Eventually Coronado was to journey more than 3,000 miles into the heartland of America: through Arizona (where a detached company discovered the Grand Canyon) and New Mexico, across the Texas plains and through Oklahoma into Kansas. They found no golden cities, only Indian pueblos and villages. In the summer of 1541, Coronado's expedition was only a few days' march from the survivors of de Soto's expedition, but they failed to meet. In 1542 Coronado returned to Mexico empty-handed with only about 100 of his men.

**De Soto's exploration of the southeastern United States, 1539–43.** In 1539 Hernando de Soto, an associate of Pizarro's in Peru, organized a well-armed expedition of 600 Spaniards and landed on the east coast of Florida, searching for the mythical Seven Cities of Gold supposed, according to Indian legend, to lie somewhere in the interior. For four years de Soto and his men fought Indians and fever, searching through Florida, Georgia, North and South Carolina. They crossed the Appalachian mountains into Tennessee and traveled through Alabama, then crossed the Mississippi River and marched through Arkansas, Oklahoma and Texas. De Soto died of fever along the way in 1542, and the survivors of his expedition ultimately reached Mexico in 1543 after terrible hardships. Of the original force, only 311 arrived in Mexico.

**Cabrillo's exploration of the California coast, 1542–43.** João Rodrigues Cabrillo, a Portuguese sailing for the King of Spain, was the first European to explore the coast of California. He visited San Diego Bay with his two ships, *San Salvador* and *Victoria*, and sailed north, stopping near present-day Los Angeles and along the coast of Santa Barbara County. In the winter of 1542 Cabrillo returned to San Diego Bay, where he died on January 3, 1543. His lieutenant, Bartolomé Ferrelo, sailed north all the way to Oregon, and at the end of the year returned to Mexico, having navigated the entire coast of California.

**Frobisher reaches Baffin Island, 1576–78.** The English began searching for a northwest passage to Asia some 30 years after Cartier had given up. In 1576 Martin Frobisher made the first of three voyages to the far north. He believed that North America was a gigantic island and that along its northernmost shore lay a passage into the Pacific Ocean. He reached Frobisher Bay and sailed westward more than 150 miles, thinking that Baffin Island was the mainland of Asia. Martin Frobisher returned to England believing that he had discovered a northwest passage to the Indies. (Here we see Frobisher's ship, the *Gabriel*, becalmed in the polar sea before a giant iceberg.)

**Drake lands in California, 1578.** Francis Drake sailed from England late in 1577, passing into the Pacific through the Straits of Magellan in the summer of 1578. He sailed north, hoping to return to the Atlantic and Europe through the passage that Frobisher claimed to have discovered. Drake went ashore in California and claimed the land (as "New Albion") for Queen Elizabeth, in defiance of earlier Spanish claims. He contin- ued north as far as the west coast of Canada, but failed to find Frobisher's passage. His return home took him across the Pacific, through the East Indies and round the Cape of Good Hope into the Atlantic. In 1580 he landed in England, having completed the second voyage round the world after Magellan's. (Here we see Drake in the stern gallery of his ship, the *Golden Hind.*)

**The Roanoke colony, 1584–87.** Sir Walter Raleigh commissioned the establishment of an English colony, to be called Virginia in honor of the Virgin Queen, Elizabeth, on the shores of North America. A reconnaissance voyage was undertaken in 1584. The first settlement, on Roanoke Island, North Carolina, was established in 1585 by Sir Richard Grenville, but unfortunately the colonists were more interested in searching for gold than in planting crops or building defenses against hostile Indians. By the summer of 1586, the colony was facing starvation. The colonists returned to England with a fleet of ships that had arrived in Virginia from the West Indies. In 1587 Raleigh sent another expedition to the abandoned colony, comprising about 110 men, women and children. They set to work repairing and rebuilding the original settlement. After four months John White, the governor, left the colony to purchase supplies in England. He never saw his colonists again. When he returned in 1590, it was only to find the colony deserted. The fate of the colonists has never been determined.

**Davis discovers Baffin Bay, 1587.** John Davis, an English captain, made three voyages (1585, 1586 and 1587) into the Arctic seas between Greenland and Baffin Island some ten years after the voyages of Martin Frobisher. He discovered Baffin Bay (1587) and visited the mouth of Hudson Strait, which enters Hudson Bay. As a result of these voyages, Davis was convinced that Baffin Bay was the northwest passage into the Pacific Ocean. (On several occasions Davis' seamen made contact with local Eskimo tribes, as we see here.)

**Oñate colonizes New Mexico, 1598.** In 1598 Don Juan de Oñate led a force of about 500 north from Mexico to secure the southwestern plains of what would become the United States of America. A weak colony was initiated at San Juan and San Gabriel. In 1601 Oñate traveled eastward along the Canadian and Arkansas Rivers. In 1604/5 he led a party that traveled all the way across Arizona. A new governor, Pedro de Peralta, established another Spanish colony on the Rio Grande in 1609, whose capital became Santa Fe (1610), a city that has been continuously occupied since that date.

**The Jamestown colonists explore Chesapeake Bay, 1607.** Jamestown, Virginia was the first permanent English colony in North America. In 1607, three ships landed at Cape Henry with 144 colonists, who explored Chesapeake Bay and the James River. They established a settlement at Jamestown, 30 miles from the mouth of the James. As in the case of the Roanoke colony, half of the settlers were dead of starvation, disease or Indian attacks by the end of the year. Reinforcements arrived during 1608, when Captain John Smith became leader of the colonists. After Smith returned to England in 1609 the colony again fell into disorder, and by the end of that winter, only 60 of the colonists were still alive. The arrival of new settlers in 1610 saved the colony from extinction, and the cultivation of tobacco for export to Europe gradually brought prosperity.

**Champlain establishes the Quebec colony, 1608.**
Samuel de Champlain made his first voyage to Canada in 1603 as a member of François Gravé's expedition, exploring the St. Lawrence River beyond the site of Montreal. He returned in 1604 and explored Nova Scotia and the coast of New England. In 1608 he established the first permanent French colony in North America at Quebec and, with his Algonquin and Montagnais Indian allies, engaged in warfare with the Iroquois near Lake Champlain. (Here we see Champlain instructing his allies in the use of the matchlock musket.) In 1612 Champlain was appointed commandant of Canada.

**Block explores New York Bay and Long Island Sound, 1610 & 1614.** Adriaen Block, a Dutch navigator, made his first voyage to America in 1610, visiting New York Bay and returning to Europe with a rich cargo of furs. In 1614, aboard his ship *Tiger*, Block returned to New York, visiting Manhattan Island, where Dutch traders and garrison troops had lived since about 1613. The *Tiger* was destroyed by fire, and Block set his crew to building a yacht which he named *Unrest*, in which he explored New York Bay. He was the first European to sail through Hell Gate, and he discovered the Housatonic and Connecticut Rivers. After sailing as far as Cape Cod, Block returned to Holland. (Here we see the yacht *Unrest* sailing off the coast of Staten Island to the delight and wonder of a party of young Indian braves.) Block Island in Long Island Sound is named for this explorer.

**Hudson discovers the Hudson River, 1609.** The English navigator Henry Hudson sailed to America in 1609 in the employ of the Dutch East India Company. In his ship the *Half Moon* he entered Chesapeake and Delaware Bays and explored New York Bay. He sailed up the river that now bears his name as far as present-day Albany before returning to Europe. Hudson made his last trip to North America in the employ of British merchants in 1610, entering Hudson Strait and sailing down Hudson Bay. He spent the winter of 1610 in James Bay, at the southern end of Hudson Bay. It was at this place in the spring of 1611 that his crew mutinied, setting Hudson, his son and several loyal crew members adrift in an open boat.

**The Pilgrims land at Plymouth, Massachusetts, 1620.**
The first European settlement in Massachusetts was made by English Pilgrims sailing in the *Mayflower* in 1620. Led by William Bradford, Miles Standish, John Carver and William Brewster, the Pilgrims arrived off the shores of Massachusetts 67 days after leaving England. Choosing an adequate harbor at Plymouth, the settlers fell to work and within a few weeks a village was laid out and houses were being erected. Sickness and hunger took many lives the first winter; however, with the help of friendly Indians, the Pilgrims survived, and six years later, when the settlement was visited by Dutch commissioners, the village consisted of strongly built houses of hewn timbers, a palisade and a fort.

**Founding of the Maryland colony, 1634.** In 1632 Cecil Calvert, Lord Baltimore, obtained from King Charles I of England authority to establish a colony in America in which Catholics could freely practice their religion. This colony was to be called Maryland, after the Queen. In February 1634 the colonists arrived at the entrance to Chesapeake Bay and then sailed south to Jamestown, where they were welcomed by the governor. From Jamestown the colonists sailed north, visited St. Clement's Island and continued up the Potomac River, where they established the settlement of St. Mary's. This became the capital of the colony of Maryland, with Leonard Calvert, brother of Cecil Calvert, as the first governor (1637).

**Johan Printz, governor of New Sweden, 1643.** Peter Minuit, the Dutch navigator who bought Manhattan from the Indians and founded New Amsterdam in 1626, was also the man who brought the first group of Swedish and Finnish settlers to North America in 1638. They explored Delaware Bay and founded their first colony on the site of the present-day city of Wilmington, naming it Fort Christina in honor of the young queen-elect of Sweden. Here we see Johan Printz, third governor of the colony of New Sweden, arriving in 1643. He served for ten years and six months with great energy but with decided severity.

**Marquette explores the Mississippi, 1673.** Jacques Marquette was a Jesuit missionary to the Canadian Indians who spent many years learning the languages of various tribes. In 1673, accompanied by Louis Jolliet, a fur trader, and five other Frenchmen, Marquette set forth from the Strait of Mackinac with two canoes to explore the entire course of the Mississippi River. Proceeding downriver to the mouth of the Ohio, the explorers were there told by Indians that it was not more than ten days' journey to the sea. They finally turned back at the mouth of the Arkansas to avoid capture by the Spanish, having satisfied themselves that the Mississippi emptied into the Gulf of Mexico. They had traveled over 2,500 miles in open canoes.

**La Salle petitions Louis XIV for permission to explore the Mississippi, 1677.** René-Robert Cavalier, Sieur de La Salle, a Frenchman living in Canada, heard of the voyage made by Marquette and Jolliet and resolved to complete their endeavor by tracing the river to its mouth. He petitioned King Louis XIV of France and received a patent allowing him to complete the exploration of the Mississippi. La Salle voyaged down the Illi-nois River in February 1682 and entered the Missis-sippi, sailing the entire length of the river to the Gulf of Mexico, which he reached in April. La Salle claimed all the territory through which the Mississippi flowed for France, and named it Louisiana in honor of the king. La Salle was killed by mutineers in Texas in 1687 when attempting to exploit his discovery.

**Cadillac founds Detroit, 1701.** Antoine de la Mothe, Sieur de Cadillac, the onetime commander of the French fortress at Mackinac in present-day Michigan, was acting under a commission from King Louis XIV when he founded a French settlement and erected a fort at Detroit on Lake Erie. The object was to control and hold the entire Great Lakes region for France. This was part of the French dream: the colony of New France, extending from the Atlantic to the Pacific, with Quebec and Detroit as its eastern and central fortresses. In 1710 Cadillac was transferred to Louisiana.

**Bering discovers Alaska and the Aleutians, 1741.**
Vitus Bering was a Dane in the service of Russia. In
1724 Tsar Peter the Great appointed him to head a
scientific expedition into the arctic regions of the Pacific. In 1728 he discovered that Asia and North America are separated by water—the strait that now bears
his name. In 1741, still in Russian service, he discovered
the Aleutian Islands and Alaska. His discoveries were
the foundation of the claim of Imperial Russia to a large
region in the northwestern part of North America,
including Alaska and, at one time, a part of California.
(Here we see Bering's ship, the *St. Peter*, driven ashore
and destroyed at Bering Island, where he died in De-
cember 1741.)

**Daniel Boone settles in Kentucky, 1775.** When Daniel Boone first came to Kentucky in 1769, the wilderness territory was considered to be part of the Colony of Virginia. After several years of exploring the area, Boone determined to found a settlement there. His first attempt, in 1773, was thwarted by Indian attacks, but in 1775 he returned, penetrated the Cumberland Gap and built a log fort at Boonesborough. Boone brought his family to Boonesborough, and his wife and daughter were the first white women in Kentucky. (Here we see Daniel Boone greeting Cherokee visitors on the Boonesborough site. Behind him stands a bark hut, much like an Indian lodge, of the type built by some of the early settlers.)

**Captain Cook explores the north Pacific coast, 1778.**
On the third of his great voyages (1776–79), English
Captain James Cook sought a passage from the north
Pacific to the North Atlantic. After discovering the
Hawaiian Islands late in 1777, his ships arrived off the
coast of Oregon the following March. Continuing
north, they stopped at Nootka Sound and sailed on to
the coast of Alaska and to the Aleutian Islands, where
they stopped at Unalaska. They sailed on north into the
Bering Sea, briefly touching on the Asiatic mainland.
The expedition returned to winter in the Hawaiian
Islands, where Captain Cook was killed in a dispute
with the natives in 1779.

**Mackenzie crosses the continent to the Pacific, 1793.** A Scottish fur trader in Canada, Alexander Mackenzie, set out from Alberta in 1789 to explore the vast wilderness of northern Canada. At the western end of Great Slave Lake he entered the river that now bears his name, and followed it 1,100 miles to the shores of the Arctic Ocean. In 1793, from the same base, Mackenzie was able to penetrate the wilderness and reach the Pacific Ocean north of the present city of Vancouver, thus having traversed the continent from east to west.

**Lewis and Clark explore the Northwest, 1804–06.**
Capt. Meriwether Lewis and Lt. William Clark of the U.S. Army were chosen by President Jefferson to explore the vast western tract of land acquired from France in 1803 (Louisiana Purchase). They headed a group of some 45 men who sailed up the Missouri River from St. Louis in May 1804. Six months later they arrived in what is now North Dakota and wintered with the Mandan Sioux. In the spring of 1805 they continued westward into the foothills of the Rocky Mountains. Launching their boats into a tributary of the Columbia River, they reached the Pacific by November. They returned across the continent, reaching St. Louis in September 1806, after an 8,000-mile journey.

**Pike maps territory in Colorado, 1806.** In 1806 Zebulon Pike of the U.S. Army (promoted to captain during the exploration) was appointed to head a geographical expedition to find the headwaters of the Red and Arkansas Rivers. He traveled through Colorado, where he discovered the Peak that is named for him, and continued west into Spanish territory in New Mexico. Pike was arrested by Spanish authorities in January 1807 and not released until the following summer. He was rewarded with a major's commission for the valuable information he had gathered. He was killed in Canada during the War of 1812.

**Fraser explores British Columbia, 1808.** In 1808 Simon Fraser, a Canadian fur trader born in Bennington (now in Vermont), set himself the task of surveying the Columbia River and finding a navigable route from the interior of western Canada to the Pacific Ocean. Setting out from Fort Macleod, Alberta, he traveled down a river he assumed to be the Columbia, but which in fact was the river that today bears his name. The journey was incredibly difficult and dangerous, and the expedition finally had to abandon their canoes. When they reached the Pacific, Fraser realized his error. In any case, the river was impassable for the fur traders' vessels. (Here we see the explorers getting their first view of the Pacific Ocean.)

**Jedediah Smith travels from Utah to California, 1826–27.** In August 1826 Jedediah Smith, trapper and mountain man, led a small party from Great Salt Lake to explore the possibility of contacting the Northwest via California. They went by way of the Wasatch Mountains, the Colorado River, the Black Mountains and the Mojave Desert. By November, they had reached the vicinity of Los Angeles, where they were halted by hostile Spanish authorities, who ordered them to leave. Returning by a different route, Smith arrived home in the summer of 1827. Smith (shown here on horseback) engaged in further journeys through 1830.